D1637720

LOVE AND SEX AND GROWING UP

NEW EDITION

Eric W. Johnson

with Illustrations by Vivien Cohen

A BANTAM SKYLARK BOOK®
NEW YORK · TORONTO · LONDON · SYDNEY · AUCKLAND

RL 4, 008-012

LOVE AND SEX AND GROWING UP
A Bantam Skylark Book

Simultaneous hardcover and Skylark editions / March 1990
Skylark Books is a registered trademark of Bantam Books,
a division of Bantam Doubleday Dell Publishing Group, Inc.
Registered in U.S. Patent and Trademark Office and elsewhere.
First edition published 1979

Library of Congress Cataloging-in-Publication Data

Johnson, Eric W.
  Love and sex and growing up.

  "A Bantam Skylark book."
  Summary: Describes the process of human reproduction from fertilization to birth, explains growth and sexual maturation, and discusses sexually transmitted diseases. Includes a glossary and review questions.
  1. Sex instruction for children. [1. Sex instruction for youth] I. Cohen, Vivien, ill. II. title.
HQ53.J6 1990   613.9'07   89-18255
ISBN 0-553-05864-9
ISBN 0-553-15800-7 (pbk.)

Published simultaneously in the United States and Canada

Bantam Books are published by Bantam Books, a division of Bantam Doubleday Dell Publishing Group, Inc. Its trademark, consisting of the words "Bantam Books" and the portrayal of a rooster, is Registered in U.S. Patent and Trademark Office and in other countries. Marca Registrada. Bantam Books, 666 Fifth Avenue, New York, New York 10103.

PRINTED IN THE UNITED STATES OF AMERICA

CWO   0 9 8 7 6 5 4 3 2

Contents

Preface

A Note to Parents and Teachers

Love and Sex and Growing Up is written for pre-teens, children between the ages of eight and twelve, who are in grades three through seven. The text is simple and direct, and the content is factual. During the several years after boys and girls learn to read and before they reach puberty, they are rightly curious about the facts of sex and love, and they are able to learn, and *enjoy* learning, a lot of information. They should have the information before they enter the turmoils of adolescence. As former Surgeon General C. Everett Koop has often noted when addressing the problem of AIDS, "Information is the best protection." He has advocated that sex education in schools begin as early as third grade.

However, sex education should be much more than antidisease education. Sexuality is not a disease! It is a wonderful and deeply important part of human life. But it also can be dangerous if expressed irresponsibly, ignorantly, or carelessly. Reading and discussing this book with your children or your students will help them avoid the dangers and understand the rewards of love and sex and growing up.

This is not a how-to book. It is not a sex book. It is a book *about* sex. It uses correct, scientific terminology, no slang. There is nothing controversial in it, unless you believe that information, plainly stated and factually illustrated, is controversial. And the book is based on sound values, which I state in the first chapter. *Love and Sex and Growing Up* does not preach. It encourages young people to learn the facts and to think about them in the light of sound values. I suggest that you, parent or teacher, read the table of contents and look at the illustrations. The illustrations are attractive, accurate, and clear. I think no one will be embarrassed by them.

There may be some parts of this book that cause you to ask, "Are fourth- and fifth-graders ready for this information?" A better question would be, "Are they ready to live responsible, productive lives without it?" Whether we parents and teachers like it or not, children are getting information and *mis*information about all of the subjects in this book. They get it from TV, magazines, movies, newspapers, comic books, and their friends—and what they get is often out of perspective and wrong. The purpose of this book is to drive out bad information with good, to replace half-truths with the facts, in order to prepare young people to make sound, responsible decisions about love and sex and growing up.

Perhaps the best place to use this book is in the home. Parents, read it yourselves and encourage your children to read it. (Possibly, your children will get it and encourage you to read it!) The book can be an excellent opening for discussing all these important matters at home. Let's face it, many families—

children and parents—have a hard time getting started talking about sex.

The book is also suitable for use as a sex education text in schools, mainly for grades four through six, although it can be useful for students as young as third-graders—and even many junior and senior high school students will learn from it (although they probably won't admit it).

As you will see, the book has a very complete index, so that anyone can look up what he or she wants to know and read about it. There is also a Word List—a glossary—that gives the pronunciations and definitions of a number of words essential to understanding the text. If readers come across a word used earlier in the book and forget its meaning, the Word List is there to help. These words are marked ■ in the text. In some cases, the Word List gives a few more facts than are included in the basic text. It also contains some useful words not found in the main body of the text.

Another feature is a short, objective multiple-choice test on the most important facts about human sexuality. Young readers will enjoy taking the test to see if they have mastered the material. And teachers may use the test in class at the end of a sex education unit.

No book can, or should try to, provide sex education complete in one volume. Even more important than book-reading is discussion with mature, enlightened people, and discussion with one's peers. Sex education must be continuous, and discussion of the sexual aspects of life must take place again and again, in different situations and with different people. I hope this book will provide the material for such education and the occasion for many such discussions.

Eric W. Johnson
Philadelphia, Pennsylvania

A Note to the Reader

This book is about love, sex, babies, marriage, and families. It is about male and female—boys and girls, men and women. It is also about growing up, something you are doing now.

This book tells you the facts about sex, plainly and clearly, with pictures and diagrams. It tries to answer all your questions. If it doesn't, though, ask your parents or your teachers. Perhaps they would like to read the book, too.

Sex

By now you have probably heard the word *sex*. You know that a person's sex is either male or female. Boys and men belong to the male sex. Girls and women belong to the female sex.

But the word *sex* means much more than female or male. It means the act in which a man and woman come together and start babies. This is called *sexual intercourse,* or "having sex." Sex can also mean the whole relationship between men and women. And it can also mean the pleasure you have in your own body as you grow up.

Human Sex: Wonderful and Dangerous

Sex is one of life's greatest pleasures. It is the way we human beings keep going by starting and bringing up more human beings.

But sex can also be dangerous. By means of sex, serious diseases can be spread from person to person, including a disease you have surely heard about, AIDS. This book explains what these diseases are and how to avoid them.

The Values on Which This Book Is Based

Before we get to the information you want and need, you may want to know the values—the principles— that have guided the writing of this book. Here they are. Do you agree with them?

- *The worth of each individual person.* You and others have infinite worth as individual people. Every person has infinite worth.
- *Consideration.* This means that you consider— think about—the needs and feelings of those around you. To do this, you have to try to know what they need and feel.

- *The family*. The best way to grow up is in a healthy, loving family. People should act in ways that will strengthen families—their own family and the families of others.
- *Responsibility*. This means thinking about the results of your actions. You keep them in mind as you decide what to do about sexual things and all other things. If the effects of your actions would be bad, you don't do them.
- *Pleasure and good feelings*. Our bodies, whether we are babies, children, grown-ups, or old people, give us good feelings. These are a valuable part of life.
- *Self-control*. Sex is a power, a force in your life, as you will find when you grow older. You must learn to control your powers, including sex, not let them control you.
- *Communication*. This means talking about things with other people—people you like, people you don't like; people in your family and out in the world. It is always good to communicate.
- *Information*. Knowing the facts, correctly, is important. Information strengthens and protects you. And that's what this book is all about! Ignorance—not knowing the facts—gets you into trouble.

How This Book Is Set Up

At the back of this book are two items that will be helpful as you read along: *a word list* and *an index*. The *Word List* tells you the meaning of some difficult words that you might want to remember. These words are marked with a symbol that looks like this:■ in the main text. In the Word List there are some other words that aren't used in the chapters in the book. They will help you understand the subject a bit better.

The *index* lists in alphabetical order all of the subjects, large and small, in the book. If there's something you want to know right away, look it up in the index, find the page, and read it. Try it now with a subject that interests you.

A Test

Also at the back of the book is a test. If you take it, you will find out whether you have learned the most important ideas and facts in the book. If you haven't learned some, you might want to read the sections again, because accurate information is important.

All right, now you're all set to read about love and sex and growing up.

Chapter 1

A Woman's Body

Living things have a beginning and end. They start life, they grow, they go on living, and they die. During their adult life, they can produce other living things like themselves—they can *re*produce.

Living things have various ways of reproducing. Human beings reproduce *sexually*. This means that both a woman and a man—a female and a male—are needed to produce a new human being. Both contribute a part to the new life.

A Woman's Sex Organs

In Figure 1 you see two drawings of parts of a woman's body. These are the parts that have to do with reproduction—that is, with making babies. They are called her *sex organs*.▪

The ▪ symbol means that the word is in the Word List, starting on page 67.

1

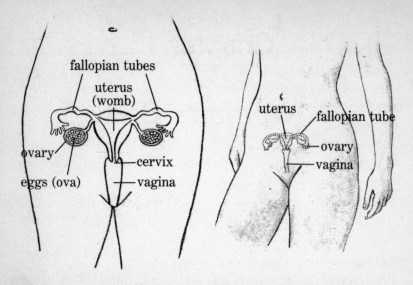

Fig. 1—Front View of Woman's Sex Organs
(scale of egg cells vastly enlarged)

Inside her body, the woman has cells that can grow into babies. These female sex cells, or eggs,■ are stored in the *ovaries*.■ The two, oval-shaped ovaries are each an inch and a half to two inches long. They are in the lowest part of the woman's abdomen■ or belly, one on each side.

When a girl baby is born, there are about 400,000 eggs already in her ovaries, many many more than she will ever need. These are not full-grown eggs. Something starts to happen to the eggs when the girl is from ten to sixteen years old. Once about every 28 days one egg ripens—becomes fully grown. This monthly ripening goes on until a woman is forty-five to fifty.

2

Ovulation

The ripe egg is pushed out of the side of the ovary with a little burst. This process is called *ovulation.*▪ The egg is caught in the end of the *fallopian tube*▪ that is nearby (see Figure 2). The egg has no way of moving itself. But inside each of the tubes are small hairs that wave in one direction. They move the egg slowly down the tube. This takes three or four days. A ripe egg is very small. Two hundred side by side would make a row only an inch long. (Another word for egg is *ovum*▪; the plural is *ova.*)

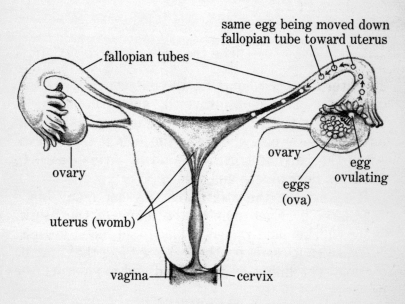

same egg being moved down fallopian tube toward uterus

fallopian tubes

ovary

ovary

egg ovulating

eggs (ova)

uterus (womb)

vagina

cervix

Fig. 2—Ovulation
(scale of egg cells vastly enlarged)

Fertilization of the Egg

The woman cannot start a baby by herself. The man must contribute, too. A male sex cell, called a *sperm*,▪ has to join with the woman's egg▪ in the tube in order to start a new life growing. If a sperm joins the egg, the egg is *fertilized*.▪ It begins immediately to grow into a baby. This growing takes about nine months. During this time the woman is *pregnant*.▪

The fertilized egg is moved on down the tube to the place where it can live while it is growing into a baby. This place is called the *uterus*▪ or *womb*▪ (pronounced "woom"). It is just about in the middle of the woman's body, where her belly is. It is the size and shape of a pear.

The Uterus

The uterus▪ is the home for the unborn baby. It also gives the baby food, warmth, and protection. It stretches as the baby grows. It has muscles to help push the baby out when it is time for it to be born. After the baby is born, the uterus shrinks back to about its normal size and shape.

The lining of the uterus has a great many blood vessels in it. Each month, the lining of the uterus grows thicker and richer in blood and blood vessels. This makes it ready for the fertilized egg that may be coming. The lining provides food and oxygen for the egg.

4

If the egg is not fertilized, the extra lining is not needed. Then, 10 to 14 days after ovulation,· this lining gradually breaks up. It is emptied out through a passage that has its outside opening between the woman's legs. This passage is called the *vagina*,· and it is about three inches long.

The monthly flow of the lining is called *menstruation*· (see Figure 3). The woman may feel cramps in her uterus when this happens, or she may not feel any pain at all. Menstruation lasts from three to seven days. A woman says she is "having her period" when she is menstruating. She wears a pad· between her legs or a tampon· in her vagina to collect the

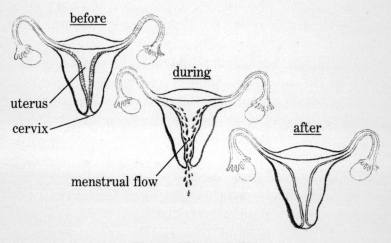

Fig. 3—Menstruation

5

flow of menstruation. She changes the pad or tampon for a clean one when it is needed, throwing the used one away. After menstruation stops, another egg begins to ripen in one of the ovaries. The lining of the uterus begins again to grow richer, ready for the next egg. This whole process is called the *monthly cycle.*■

But if the egg has been fertilized and has started to grow in the uterus, then there is no menstruation. No new egg comes from the ovaries until after the baby is born.

Three Openings

There are three openings between a woman's legs (see Figure 4). The front one is for the flow of urine. It is called the *urethra.*■ The middle one is the opening of the *vagina.*■ The back one is for bowel movements and is called the *anus.*■ (Of course, a man has an anus, too.)

The vagina has several uses. It is a passage for menstrual flow, as we have just learned. It stretches to let a baby through as it is born. It is the part of a woman's body in which the man places sperms,■ one of which may fertilize the egg.

The sex organs■ on the surface of the woman's body are called her *genitals.*■ The genitals have three parts. They are the opening of the vagina, the folds of skin (called *labia*■) that surround and protect this opening, and the *clitoris*■ (see Figure 4). The clitoris is a very sensitive organ, one-sixth to

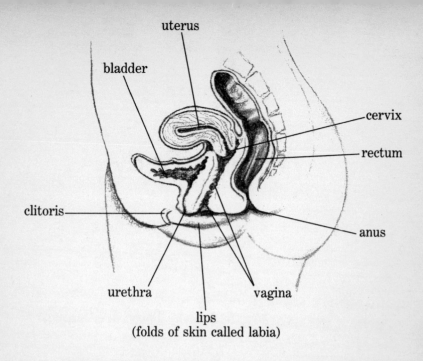

Fig. 4—Side View of Some of a Woman's Organs

one-half-inch long. As a girl grows older, she will have strong feelings of sexual pleasure in her clitoris. But the clitoris is not necessary for reproduction, only for pleasure.

Chapter 2

A Man's Body

A man has sex organs,▪ too. They are shown in Figure 5.

A Man's Sex Organs

The man's sex cells, or *sperms*,▪ are made by two organs about the same size and shape as a woman's ovaries.▪ They are the man's *testicles*.▪ The testicles are carried outside the man's body rather than inside it. They are in a pouch of crinkly skin that hangs between his legs. This pouch is called the *scrotum*.▪

The man's sex cell looks like a very small tadpole (see Figure 6). The body of the cell is the reproductive part. The tail makes the sperm swim. It wriggles.

The sperm is different from the woman's egg (ovum▪) in several ways. It is much smaller. One hundred thousand sperms would fit in the same space

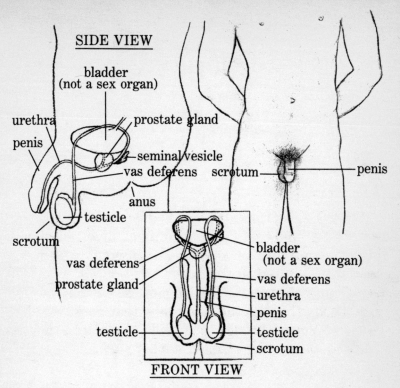

SIDE VIEW

bladder
(not a sex organ)

urethra

penis

prostate gland

seminal vesicle

vas deferens

scrotum

penis

anus

testicle

scrotum

vas deferens

prostate gland

bladder
(not a sex organ)

vas deferens

urethra

penis

testicle

testicle

scrotum

FRONT VIEW

Fig. 5—A Man's Sex Organs
(and bladder, which is not a sex organ)

as one egg. The sperm can move itself along by
lashing its tail. The egg cannot move itself at all.
New sperms are always being made in a man's testicles. A woman's ovaries do not make any new eggs.
They store the eggs she already had when she was
born.

From the testicles, the sperms move into two tubes,
each called a *vas deferens*.▪ They lead the sperms up
into the man's body from the scrotum. (See Figure 5.)

9

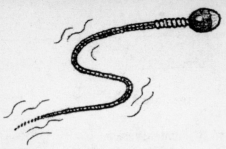

Fig. 6—A Sperm

After they go through the vas deferens, the sperms mix with a fluid that helps keep them alive and vigorous. The mixture of sperms and fluid is called *semen*.■ It is stored in two sacs, the *seminal vesicles*■ (see Figure 5 again). The semen passes out of the man's body through the same tube that goes from his *bladder*■ down through his penis. This tube is the man's *urethra*.■ (The bladder is where urine is stored.)

The Penis and Scrotum

The man's most visible sex organs■ are his *penis*■ and *scrotum*.■ These are his *genitals*.■ The penis in a grown man is three to four inches long. It is somewhat thicker than the man's thumb. It hangs down from his groin■ between his legs, in front of his scrotum. The man urinates through his penis. He also uses his penis to spurt semen■ inside the woman's vagina■ during sexual intercourse.■

The ■ symbol means that the word is in the Word List, starting on page 67.

Semen and urine can never mix together because a special valve keeps them from passing out of the man's urethra at the same time.

Circumcision

When a boy is born, the end of his penis■ is covered by a fold of skin. This is his *foreskin*.■ Shortly after his birth, the baby's foreskin may be cut off by a doctor or specialist. This is a very simple operation. It is called *circumcision*.■ Among Jews and Muslims it is done for religious reasons. Figure 7 shows the difference between an uncircumcised penis and a circumcised one.

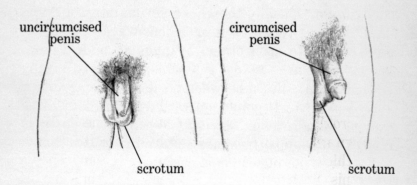

uncircumcised penis

circumcised penis

scrotum

scrotum

Fig. 7—Penis and Scrotum

11

Chapter 3

How a Baby Starts Growing

A new human life starts when one of a man's sperms■ joins a woman's egg. This can happen when a man and a woman *mate* with each other, when they have *sexual intercourse*.■ Usually they have sexual intercourse in bed. They get ready for it in various ways—by speaking lovingly to each other, by hugging and kissing. When the man is ready, his penis,■ which is usually limp and hangs down between his legs, becomes much longer and stiff. It points outward from his body. This change is called an *erection*.■ When the woman is ready, her vagina■ becomes soft and moist so that it can receive the man's penis easily.

Sexual Intercourse

The man then puts his penis■ into the woman's vagina.■ The man and the woman move back and forth together, and after a time the penis spurts about a

12

teaspoonful of semen■ into the woman's vagina. The sperms■ can then swim to meet the egg■ (see Figure 8). This mating of man and woman is called *sexual intercourse.*■

The spurting out of semen—*ejaculation*■—is the *climax*■ of sexual intercourse for a man. The woman has a climax, too. The walls of her vagina contract several times, but there is no sudden discharge of fluid. In both men and women, the climax gives great pleasure.

Sexual intercourse is a private experience that a man and a woman share. It can make them feel very close, besides serving as the way to bring the sperm to the egg so that a new life can start. This is why sexual intercourse is also called lovemaking.

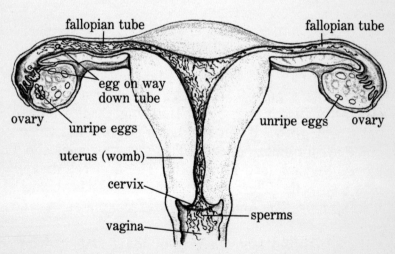

fallopian tube   fallopian tube

egg on way
down tube

ovary   unripe eggs   unripe eggs   ovary

uterus (womb)—

cervix—

—sperms

vagina—

Fig. 8—Sperms on Way to Egg After Sexual Intercourse
(scale of egg cells vastly enlarged)

13

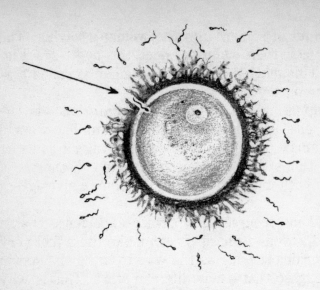

Fig. 9—One Sperm Enters Egg
A baby is conceived.

Human Cells

When the egg and a sperm■ join, *conception*■ takes place. (See Figure 9.) The egg and sperm form one cell, a *fertilized*■ egg. From this single cell a human baby will grow. When the baby is born, it will be made up of millions of cells. This growth comes about by cell division (see Figure 10). The first cell divides into two cells. Then each of the new cells divides, making four. The four cells divide, making eight, and so on.

The fertilized egg, already dividing and growing, continues to be moved along the woman's fallopian tube.■ It reaches the uterus■ three or four days

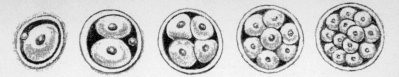

Fig. 10—Cell Division—Fertilized Egg Begins to Grow

after leaving the ovary.▪ It settles into the lining of the uterus. It keeps on dividing. At first each cell is the same as all the others, but gradually the cells take on special jobs. Some cells will make the skin of the new baby. Others will make its muscles, brain, nerves, and bones. Still others will make other internal organs.

Development of the New Life

For about the first two months, the developing cells are called the *embryo*.▪

At one month, the embryo is about a quarter of an inch long. After two months, the embryo is called a *fetus*.▪ In Figure 11, the human embryo, then fetus,▪ is shown at two, three, and four months. At four months, the fetus is six inches long and weighs a third of a pound. It can move its arms and legs. The mother can feel these movements. You can see in Figures 11, 12, and 13 how it develops. By six months the fetus looks quite a lot like a baby, except that it does not yet have any "baby fat."

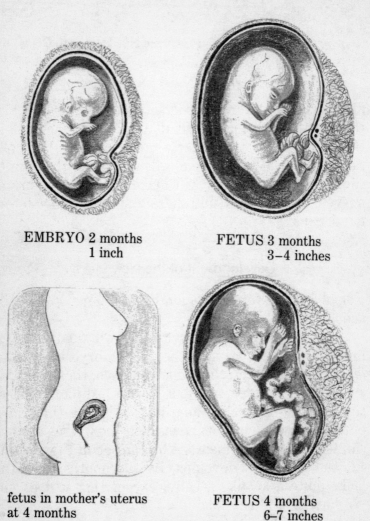

EMBRYO 2 months
1 inch

FETUS 3 months
3–4 inches

fetus in mother's uterus
at 4 months

FETUS 4 months
6–7 inches

Fig. 11—Development of the Embryo, Then Fetus

A baby born before six months rarely survives. Its organs (which include its heart, lungs, and stomach) are not fully made. They may not be able to work properly to keep the baby alive. A baby born at six months has a chance to live, but it needs very good, special care. It may weigh about two pounds. If a six-month baby is born in a hospital, it is placed in an

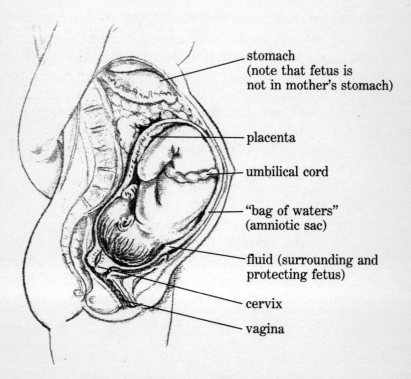

stomach
(note that fetus is
not in mother's stomach)

placenta

umbilical cord

"bag of waters"
(amniotic sac)

fluid (surrounding and
protecting fetus)

cervix

vagina

Fig. 12—Baby Almost Ready for Birth

17

incubator■ until it is big and strong enough to live without special protection. The incubator keeps the baby warm and protected almost the way the uterus■ does. Babies born early are called *premature*.■ Most babies stay in the mother's uterus for the full term of nine months. They weigh about six to eight pounds when they are born.

Growing in the Uterus

During the time the embryo■ (and then the fetus■) is in the uterus■ (*not* the stomach!), it must have food and oxygen to live and grow. It cannot eat or breathe for itself because it is floating in fluid inside a sac (see Figure 12). This is to protect it from bumps. The embryo receives food and oxygen from its mother through a sort of tube attached to its abdomen■ (see Figure 12 again). The tube is called the *umbilical cord*.■ The cord goes from the embryo's abdomen to the *placenta*,■ a spongy collection of small blood vessels. The placenta is attached to the wall of the mother's uterus. Blood in the placenta picks up food and oxygen from the mother's blood. These go through the cord to the embryo (or fetus). Waste from the embryo goes back the other way and passes across to the mother. The blood of the mother and the blood of the embryo or fetus do not mix. The developing baby makes its own blood.

Chapter 4

The Baby Is Born

While the baby grows in the uterus,■ the uterus stretches to give it room. The woman is *pregnant*■ during this time. (See Figure 13.) Her abdomen■ grows bigger, and she looks fatter. Her breasts grow

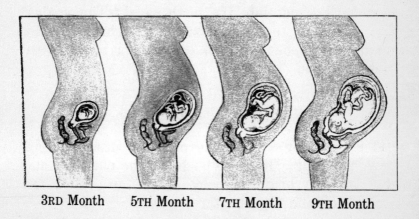

3RD Month   5TH Month   7TH Month   9TH Month

**Fig. 13—Pregnancy—
Development of Baby in Mother's Uterus**

larger. They are getting ready to give milk for the baby when it is born.

Labor and Birth

When the time comes for the baby to be born, the mother's uterus■ stops stretching. Its strong muscles begin to contract. They draw together time after time in a sort of rhythm. This is hard work for the mother. It can hurt because the muscles often have to keep working hard for a long time. The contracting of the muscles is called *labor*.■ Labor may last anywhere from a few minutes to more than a day.

Figures 14 and 15 show how a baby is born. Usually the baby has turned so that it is head-down in the uterus. As the muscles of the mother's uterus contract, the baby breaks through the bag of waters that holds it. The neck of the uterus stretches open, and the baby's head pushes out into the birth canal.■ The vagina■ also stretches to let the baby through. The baby finally comes out through the vagina between its mother's legs.

Right After the Baby Is Born

After the baby's birth, the mother's uterus■ keeps on contracting. This is to push out the placenta■ and the sac that held the baby. These are called the *afterbirth*,■ and they are thrown away.

You remember that the fetus in its mother's uterus

20

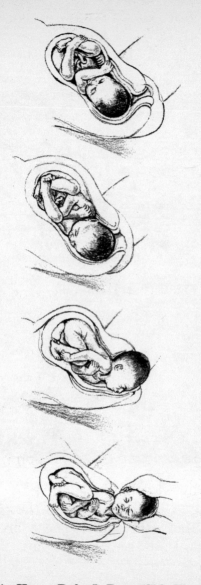

Fig. 14—How a Baby Is Born (Side View)

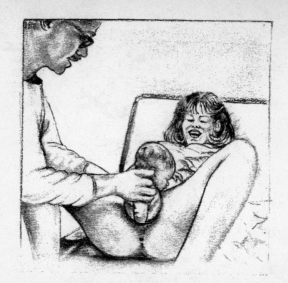

Fig. 15 (Part I)—Another View of Birth

Fig. 15 (Part II)—Just After Birth

22

was not able to breathe and eat for itself. It got its food and oxygen from the mother through the umbilical cord.■ When the baby is born, it starts to breathe and it can suck to get food. The cord is no longer needed. Shortly after the baby is born, the cord is tied and cut by the doctor or nurse who is helping at the birth. Cutting it does not hurt the baby or the mother, because there are no nerves in the cord. Your *navel*■ or belly button is the place where your umbilical cord was attached to you.

Brothers and sisters, and fathers and mothers, too, think of a baby as being pretty and cute. Often when they see a baby who has just been born, they are disappointed. The baby's head may have been pushed out of shape when it was born. Or the baby may look red and lumpy and even angry, not at all pretty. After a few days the head goes back into shape, the skin becomes a normal color, and the baby grows used to breathing and eating independently. Then the baby begins to look more the way we think babies should look.

After the baby is born, the mother's breasts begin to produce milk. The newborn baby gets food for its first few months from just sucking milk. This comes either from the mother's breasts or from a bottle. The milk given in a bottle usually is cow's milk with other things added to make it as much like mother's milk as possible. This is called *formula*.

After the baby's birth, the mother's abdomen■ is suddenly much smaller. Soon, she looks about the way she did before she was pregnant.■ Her breasts may be larger because they are providing milk for the baby. It takes about six weeks for her uterus to go all the way back to its normal shape and size.

23

Chapter 5

What You Get from Your Mother and Your Father—Heredity

Whom will the new baby look like? In a family, one child may look a lot like the mother and another child may look more like the father. Some children look like a mixture of both parents. Perhaps you have been told that you have your mother's eyes, your father's mouth. The resemblance may go farther back—a child may look or even act like one of its grandparents.

Your Heredity

What you get from your mother and your father— your characteristics—is called your *heredity*.■ It includes what your body will look like—whether you will be short or tall, light- or heavy-boned, and so on. Heredity decides your eye color, your skin and hair color, and whether you will have straight or curly hair. Heredity may also include some of your talents—for music, sports, art, numbers, words, or work with your hands, for example.

But heredity does not decide everything. Exactly how tall or heavy you will be depends partly on what kind of food, rest, and health care you have. Heredity does not decide what you will do with your talents and abilities, either. That depends a great deal on what happens to you after you are born. It depends on whether you are close to other people with the same talents and interests who can encourage you. It depends on how hard you try, on how good your teachers and coaches are, on how much time you can spend learning, and on how good a learner you are.

How Heredity Works—Genes

Let's see how heredity■ works. Very, very small parts of the egg■ cell and the sperm■ cell determine what the heredity of the new baby will be. These are called the baby's *genes*.■ The baby gets half its genes from its mother and half from its father. A gene in the father's sperm (the one that fertilized the egg) determines whether the baby will be a girl or a boy.

Each child in a family inherits different genes from its mother and different genes from its father. Which genes it receives depends on chance. This is one reason that brothers and sisters are different in many ways. The only exception is in the case of some twins—two babies born at the same time.

Twins

Twins can be started in two ways. (See Figure 16.) Some twins are started from one fertilized■ egg. The egg divides into two separate parts. Then each of these parts develops into a baby. Finally twins are born. The twins are almost exactly the same, because they have come from the same egg and the same sperm. Both inherit the same genes■ from their parents. They are called *identical* twins.

Perhaps you know twins who look so much alike that people are confused and cannot tell which one they are talking to. Those are identical twins. Identical twins are always the same sex.

Other twins are started when there are two eggs in the woman's fallopian tubes■ at about the same time. Each egg is fertilized by a separate sperm. The two fertilized eggs then grow at the same time in the mother's uterus.■ The two babies are born at about the same time. But they are no more alike than ordinary brothers and sisters. They have received different sets of genes from their parents. They may

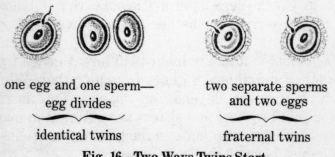

one egg and one sperm—
egg divides

two separate sperms
and two eggs

identical twins   fraternal twins
Fig. 16—Two Ways Twins Start

be the same sex or they may be a boy and a girl. They are called *fraternal* twins.

Triplets, quadruplets, or quintuplets are born when three, four, or five babies have grown in the uterus at the same time. These brothers and sisters may be identical or fraternal. Or there may be some of each. Birth of more than two babies at once is very unusual.

Chapter 6

Growing Up:
From Birth to Age Five

New babies are pretty helpless. They can sleep. They can breathe. They can move their arms and legs, and they can see shapes and hear sounds. They can suck, they can cry, and they can urinate and empty their bowels. They depend on their mothers and fathers for almost everything: food, warmth, cleanliness, and loving.

New babies like their stomachs to be full of milk, and they like to be warm and dry. They like to be cuddled, rocked, patted, handled. They drink milk by their own sucking. They are likely to find that sucking is fun even when they are full, that cuddling is nice even when they are warm. Babies suck their thumbs, their clothes, their toys. They try every new thing in their mouths. They like to be picked up and held when they are awake.

As Babies Grow Older

As babies grow older, they learn many new things. One thing they learn is that they are separate people.

They can tell that they are people and their mothers are other people. They can tell that toys, bed, and food are things which are not part of themselves. When babies are about one year old they learn to walk. At about two, they start to talk. They begin to understand what other people want. They can make others understand what they want.

When they are very young, babies *take*. They take food, they take love—and they give nothing back, except smiles or gurgles. When they can talk and walk, they can start to give as well as take. They like to hand things to their mothers or fathers and hear them say "Thank you." They hug their mothers and fathers to show affection the same way the parents have been showing theirs. They like the give-and-take of rough-housing. They are probably very proud of what they give and proud of being able to give.

The Years Three to Five

Babies keep growing and learning. They begin to know people outside the family. They learn to play and to share. They see that other people have needs and rights, too. During the years from about three to five, children start to make friends their own age. They may go to nursery or play school.

Boys and girls around this age realize for the first time a very important thing. They realize that boys and girls look different. A boy may see his little sister or a girl playmate going to the bathroom, taking a bath, having diapers changed, or swimming. He sees that she has no penis▪ and scrotum.▪ Since up to this time he has learned only about himself, he may think there is something wrong with the little girl.

In the same way, a girl may see a boy going to the bathroom, taking a bath, having his diapers changed, or swimming. She sees that he has a penis and scrotum between his legs, things she does not have. She may wonder why she does not have them.

Learning About Bodies, Male and Female

Both the boy and the girl learn that they are made differently because they are going to grow up to be different. They learn that is the way things are supposed to be. The boy will grow up to be a man and probably a father. His penis■ and scrotum■ are right for him. The girl is going to be a woman and probably a mother. Her vagina■ and other sex organs■ are right for her.

Infants and young children are likely to discover that handling their genitals■ feels good. They may touch their genitals in order to have this pleasant feeling. Some do it often, some not so often.

Small children are growing ready for school and lessons. But before school they learn a great deal, maybe even more than they will learn at school. They learn about people—about themselves and their families and their playmates. They learn about how their world works and how people are related to each other.

The ■ symbol means that the word is in the Word List, starting on page 67.

Chapter 7

Growing Up: From Six to Twelve

Boys and girls turn to new things in the years from six on. Their world is getting bigger. They go to school. They are away from home and from their families much of the time. They are busy learning about things outside themselves most of the time. Their bodies are not changing a great deal but are growing slowly and steadily, preparing for the changes that will come in the teen years.

Boys and Girls Playing

Up to now it has not mattered much whether playmates were girls or boys. Now, though, boys are likely to want to play with boys, girls with girls. Boys may tease girls; girls may chase boys. There may sometimes be some special boy and girl friends. But most of the time boys want to play games, start projects, or rough-house with other boys. Girls usually want to work and talk and play with other girls.

Some girls, however, prefer being with boys and playing what people think of as boys' games. They used to be called *tomboys*. These girls probably also have girl friends. Some boys are not so sports-minded as others, and they may enjoy being with girls, though they probably also have some boy friends, too.

These girls and boys are somewhat different from most of their classmates in what they like or are willing to do. They may feel lonely sometimes, and their classmates may tease them. But times and ideas are changing, and there are fewer and fewer activities just for boys or just for girls. Girls play on baseball teams. Boys enjoy cooking and knitting. Generally, as everyone grows up, these differences seem even less important.

Chapter 8

Growing Up: Teenager to Adulthood

When boys and girls are between ten or eleven and fifteen or sixteen years old, their bodies begin to change quite rapidly. These changes are very important. They come at a time called *puberty*.▪

Boys' Development

Let's take a boy first and see what happens to him at puberty (see Figure 17). Usually when he is around thirteen or fourteen (but it can be two or three years earlier or later), he begins to grow hair around and above his penis.▪ This is called *pubic hair*.▪ He also begins to grow more hair on his body: under his arms, on his arms and legs, sometimes on his chest and back, and finally, on his face (his mustache and beard). Also, the boy's voice box grows larger. This is what makes his voice change to the deeper voice of a man.

33

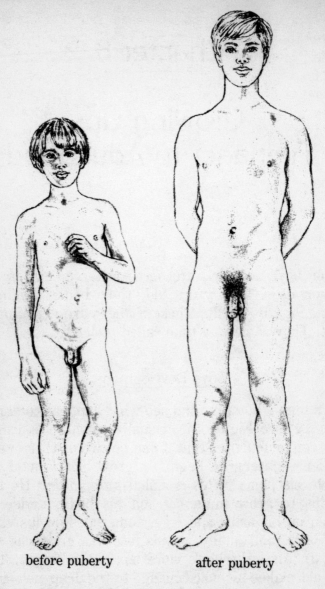

before puberty   after puberty

Fig. 17—A Boy Before and After Puberty

34

For a couple of years the boy grows taller much faster than he has grown before. His shoulders grow wider, his hips and waist slim down. The features of his face—nose, mouth, chin—grow bigger. His skin becomes oilier and he may be bothered by pimples, or *acne*.■

At puberty,■ too, a boy's genitals■ become larger. His testicles■ begin to make sperms.■ He is physically able to become the father of children even though he is not grown-up enough to marry. He is probably not yet mature enough to help build a family, to *be* a father. And it would be very hard for him and a young wife to earn all the money they would need to support a family, since there are not many jobs for young people and those that are for young people pay very little.

At puberty a boy begins to spurt out semen■ from his penis. The word for this is *ejaculation*.■ Sometimes this happens when he is handling his penis. This is called *masturbation*.■ You will read more about this later. Sometimes ejaculation happens when the boy is in close contact with a girl. And sometimes it happens at night, often when he is dreaming about girls or sex. These night-time ejaculations are often called "wet dreams."■

When a boy first ejaculates semen, no matter how he does it, it means that he is probably physically able to become a father.

Adolescence in Boys

The time that starts with puberty* and ends with adulthood is called *adolescence.** In adolescence many boys begin to be interested in girls in a new way. They like to be around girls. They want the girls to notice them and to think they are fun to be with.

Boys begin to think more than they did about how they look. They may comb their hair and choose their clothes carefully. They may look in their mirrors frequently. To their younger brothers and sisters this may seem pretty silly, but it is a sign that these male adolescents are growing up.

Girls' Development

A girl is likely to reach puberty* when she is twelve or thirteen, though it may be a lot earlier or later (see Figure 18). The girl's breasts become noticeably larger. Pubic hair* begins to grow around and above her genitals.* Hair also grows under her arms, on her arms and legs, and sometimes in a faint mustache on her upper lip. The girl's voice box grows bigger, too, giving her voice the fuller sound of a woman's, but this is not as noticeable as it is in boys. The girl's skin also becomes oilier, and she may be troubled by *acne.**

Menstruation

At puberty there are also changes in a girl's sex organs. She begins to menstruate,* as explained on page 5 and shown in Figure 3. Her ovaries* start to produce ripe

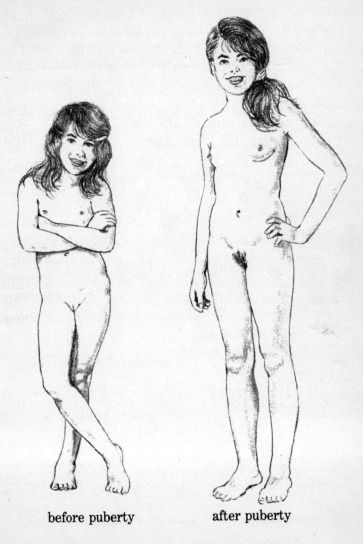

before puberty   after puberty

Fig. 18—A Girl Before and After Puberty

37

eggs, sometimes at the time she starts to menstruate, sometimes earlier, or often one or two years later.

A girl can do several things to be ready for her first menstruation. She can talk with her mother or another woman about menstruation. She can buy the supplies she will need: *menstrual pads*.▪ These pads are worn between the legs to absorb the menstrual flow (see Figure 19).

Another way to absorb the flow is to use *tampons*▪ (see Figure 19). Tampons are absorbent rolls

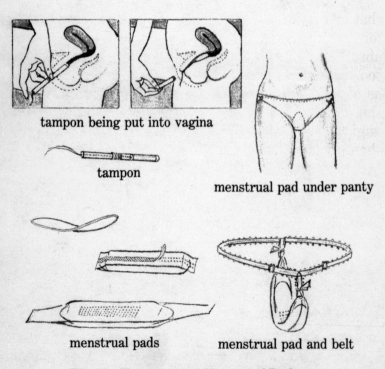

tampon being put into vagina

tampon

menstrual pad under panty

menstrual pads

menstrual pad and belt

Fig. 19—Tampons and Menstrual Pads

**Fig. 20—Different Types of
Hymen at Opening to the Vagina**

that are worn inside the vagina. The menstrual flow for the first day or two may be too heavy to be absorbed by a tampon, so that a pad may be needed, too. Some girls are not able to use a tampon as easily as others. This is because a thin piece of flesh called the *hymen*,■ which partly closes the entrance of the vagina, may leave a smaller opening in some girls than in others (see Figure 20).

During the early part of her menstrual period, a girl may want to cut down on strenuous games and play. But mostly she can lead her usual life. She may also feel a little tired and somewhat cranky. These feelings go away after a day or two.

Adolescence in Girls

In adolescence■ most girls become more interested in boys. They want to be with boys and learn to know them as friends. Girls are likely to whisper and giggle about boys. They begin to care a lot about how they look. They may take hours fixing their hair and choosing their clothes. They may start to use makeup.

Teenage girls, like teenage boys, may seem pretty silly to their younger brothers and sisters. But the girls are really learning about boys. They are learning how to get along with boys and how to attract them. It is helpful to know these things as they grow up.

Girls usually reach puberty* a year or two before boys do. This shows in their earlier body changes, their earlier growing spurts, and their earlier interest in the other sex. For most girls, the ovaries* do not begin to produce ripe eggs until some time after the girl reaches puberty and begins to menstruate. A few girls, however, can become pregnant even before they first menstruate. There is no single pattern of growth.

Masturbation

After puberty* both boys and girls feel more pleasure from handling their genitals.* A young person may handle or rub his or her own genitals on purpose to have pleasure. This is called *masturbation.* Masturbation for these young people is a very common part of growing up and discovering their own bodies and the feelings their bodies can give them.

Masturbation is harmless to the body. Yet many boys and girls are told that it is bad, or that it is bad for them. Many adults have been taught and believe

40

that it is harmful. Some religions say that masturbation is a sin. If young people feel that masturbation is bad or sinful, they may try to avoid it, and thus avoid the guilty feeling. But I emphasize that there is no harm from masturbating except the guilt it makes some people feel. (There is no harm from *not* masturbating either.) Each person will decide about masturbation for him- or herself. Like all other sexual activity, it is a private matter.

Some Difficulties of Adolescence

Adolescence■ is not always an easy time for boys and girls. Their bodies are going through big changes. These changes do not all come at the same time. This can make a boy or girl awkward and clumsy for a while.

One thing that sometimes makes adolescence difficult is that young people reach puberty■ at different ages (see Figures 21 and 22). One boy may start his body changes when he is eleven. Another may not begin until he is fifteen or sixteen. The second boy may worry when he is thirteen or fourteen because his body is still like a child's body, and his genitals■ are not as fully developed as the first boy's. One girl may start to menstruate■ when she is ten, another not until she is sixteen. The second may worry when she is thirteen or fourteen because her body, and especially her breasts, are not as fully developed as the first girl's.

All these boys and girls are normal. The truth is that

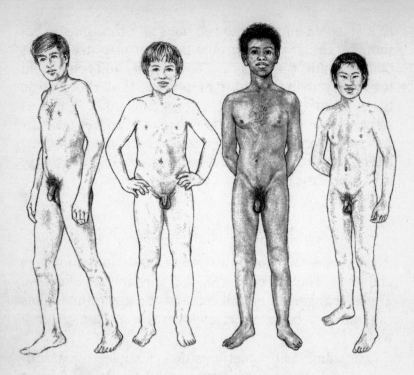

Fig. 21—Four Teenage Boys of the Same Age
(Some have reached puberty, some have not.)

people just develop differently. Even so, friends who reach puberty at different rates may not understand each other. One wants to date, the other hates the idea, and so on. Somebody is likely to feel hurt or left out. They will all catch up by their late teens, but there will be some hard times for some of them first. It is a little easier if they understand what is going on and know that it is going to happen that way.

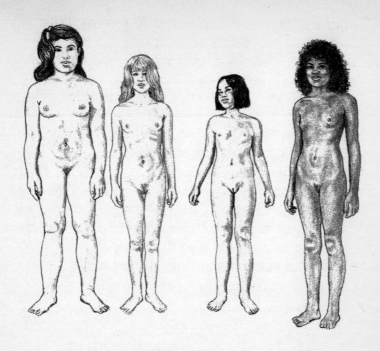

Fig. 22—Four Teenage Girls of the Same Age
(Some have reached puberty, some have not.)

Becoming an Adult

The last step in a person's growth is becoming an adult. Adults, unless they are handicapped in some way, are able to take care of themselves, to go to work, to have families of their own, and to support them.

In our society this step comes anywhere between eighteen and twenty-five or even later. It depends on the person and the kind of life he or she expects to lead. More and more people are going on to college and graduate school after high school, and this delays the time when they go to work. These people generally depend on their families longer than young people who start jobs right after high school.

Adults' bodies have stopped growing. Girls reach this point in their teens, boys in their early twenties. They will be no taller or broader-boned, though they may gain some weight. (One small child said to me, "A grown-up is a person who has stopped growing on both ends and started growing in the middle.")

Chapter 9

Homosexuality

Some men are sexually attracted to other men. Some women are sexually attracted to other women. This is *homosexuality*.▪ (The first part of the word comes from the Greek word *homos*, meaning "same.") Homosexual males are often called *gay*.▪ Female homosexuals are also called gay but more often *lesbians*.▪ (The word comes from the Greek island of Lesbos. In ancient times many women who lived there enjoyed a homosexual way of life.)

People sometimes ask, "What causes a person to be homosexual?" There is no simple answer to the question. (You could ask, "What causes people to be *heterosexual*?"▪—sexually attracted to people of the other sex. There's no simple answer to that question either.) But scientists generally agree that being homosexual is not a matter of choice. Homosexuality is established very early in life, perhaps even before birth.

Perhaps about 10 percent of people are homosexual, probably more men than women. Gay and lesbian people feel strongly that they should have the same rights as anyone else.

Recently, because of the disease AIDS* (see pages 54–58), some people have come to fear homosexuals, since they are more likely than heterosexuals to carry the disease. This fear is not based on fact. There are two ways to get AIDS from a homosexual person. One is to choose to have sex with him or her. The other is sharing needles while injecting drugs.

There is a growing acceptance of gay and lesbian people in our society. However, for religious and other reasons, the acceptance is far from complete. Therefore, many homosexuals hide the fact that they are gay or lesbian.

Can you tell who is homosexual by looking at a person? No. Homosexuals, unless they choose to identify themselves, look like everyone else. They are found in all areas of life, from football players and truck drivers to artists and scientists and business managers.

Chapter 10

Sexual Intercourse Does Not Always Make Babies

To have babies is not the only reason why men and women have sexual intercourse.■ There are many other important reasons. Suppose a man and a woman are very much in love. This can mean many things.

Some Reasons for Having Sexual Intercourse

Having sexual intercourse■ can mean that a man and a woman like and respect each other. It can mean that they want to make life good for each other, to feel responsible for each other always. Being in love can mean the man and woman want to feel very close to each other, to share their lives and thoughts and feelings and bodies very deeply with each other.

For this man and woman, having sexual intercourse can be one of the best and most enjoyable ways of expressing and strengthening their feeling for each

47

other. Sex together gives them great pleasure. They have a strong, warm feeling for each other. This feeling spreads to things outside themselves, too. It makes them feel better about their family, their friends, their work, their whole lives.

Why Not Have Babies?

The man and woman often may want to have intercourse and still be sure that they will not start a baby. This could be because they are not yet ready to take care of a family, because they already have as many children as they can take care of, or because they want to let one baby grow to a certain age before they have another. Or both the mother and the father may be working, and neither wants to be kept home by having a baby to care for.

Family Planning

Therefore, many couples plan for smaller families. This is called *family planning*▪ or *birth control*.▪ Doctors have found methods that couples can use so that they can have intercourse and usually not have babies. These are methods of *contraception*.▪ There are a number of reliable ways of keeping the sperm▪ and egg from joining together. However, none of them is foolproof, especially if they are not used carefully, intelligently, and exactly according to instructions.

One way to stop the sperm■ and egg■ from meeting is to block the path of the sperm. To do this, before a couple has intercourse, the man may put on a rubber cap, or *condom*,■ over his penis,■ or the woman may put a different sort of cap, called a *diaphragm*,■ over the opening of her uterus■ (see Figure 23).

Another way to avoid conception is for the woman to take *birth control pills*.■ These pills stop eggs from ripening and coming out of her ovaries.■

Or a couple can simply not have intercourse around the time they figure the woman's ovaries are likely to produce a ripe egg—the time she *ovulates*.■ This is called *Natural Family Planning*.■ It is called "natural" because no artificial means are used. It is done by the woman studying her own body very carefully and keeping careful records. For most people, this requires a training course from a specialist if it is to work well.

Yet another method of contraception is to have an object, called an *IUD*■ (*intrauterine device*), placed in the woman's uterus (see Figure 23). The IUD prevents the egg from settling into the lining of the uterus.

A couple is usually helped by their doctor or a specialist in family planning to choose and use properly one of these ways of avoiding having a baby. Doctors and scientists are constantly seeking easier, better methods of contraception.

The ■ symbol means that the word is in the Word List, starting on page 67.

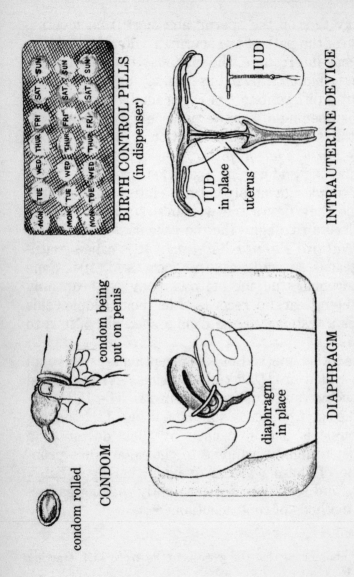

BIRTH CONTROL PILLS
(in dispenser)

INTRAUTERINE DEVICE

IUD

IUD in place

uterus

condom being put on penis

condom rolled

CONDOM

diaphragm in place

DIAPHRAGM

Fig. 23—Four Methods of Contraception
Condom, birth control pills, diaphragm, and intrauterine device (IUD)

Abortion

Another method not to have a child is *abortion.*■
A woman knows she is pregnant because she is no
longer menstruating. If she and her mate used a
contraceptive, they know that it has failed. Or they
took a chance and she got pregnant.■ If they decide
not to have the child, the woman goes to a clinic
or a hospital and has an abortion. It is a simple
procedure, usually. If it is done early in the pregnancy, the risks are slight. It is less dangerous
than giving birth to a baby—and that, too, is very
safe.

The most common method of abortion is to use
special equipment that sucks the embryo,■ placenta,■
and other materials out of the woman's uterus.■

Some people feel very strongly against abortion.
They say that it is killing a human life. Other people
feel that a woman has the right to decide what she
does with her own body. They say that the embryo or
fetus■ is not a "person" until it is born.

One thing is sure: Abortion is a very poor method
of family planning.

Sterilization

It is possible for a man or a woman who does not
wish ever to have any more children to be *sterilized.*
To sterilize a man, a doctor ties and cuts the vas
deferens■ (see Figure 5, page 9) so that no sperms■
can pass through. To sterilize a woman, a doctor ties
and cuts the fallopian tubes■ (see Figure 1, page 2),

51

so that neither eggs nor sperms can pass. Sterilization■ does not prevent a man or woman from enjoying sexual intercourse■ fully.

Adopting a Child

Most couples who want children can have them. But there are some men and women who are not able to have children, perhaps because their reproductive organs have been damaged by disease or did not develop as they should. Such couples may adopt children. This is called *adoption*.■ They may take into their family children whose natural parents cannot take care of them. Adopted children belong to the new parents. They are loved just as other children are loved by their parents.

Chapter 11

How Sexual Activity Can Spread Disease*

Earlier in the book, I said that human sex is wonderful *and* dangerous. We have already discussed the pleasures and importance of sex. Now it is time to talk about the several serious diseases that can be spread by sexual activity.

Sexually Transmitted Diseases—STDs

These diseases are called *sexually transmitted diseases* (STDs). To transmit means to pass from one person to another. Another name for STDs is *venereal disease* (VD). The word *venereal* comes from Venus, the name of the Roman goddess of love. When

---

*The facts in this chapter have been checked by Lawrence S. Weisberg, MD, Assistant Professor of Medicine, University of Medicine and Dentistry of New Jersey/Robert Wood Johnson School of Medicine, Camden, New Jersey.

you are older and considering whether or not you should have sexual intercourse," you should learn the details about STDs and what to do if you think you have one—how to get treated and cured. If people do not get treated, the diseases may cause serious problems. The problems are pain, serious damage to the body, the inability to have children, and even death. One sexually transmitted disease, AIDS, up till now always causes death.

The Most Common STDs

The most common and serious STDs, listed here in alphabetical order, are AIDS," gonorrhea," herpes," non-gonococcal urethritis, syphilis, trichomonas, and urethritis. Facts about each of them are given in the Word List. Look them up if you are interested. Actually, AIDS is not yet one of the most common STDs. But it is spreading rapidly and may soon be. It always causes death. As yet, there is no cure for it. Because of its growth and danger—and because of the great fear it causes among people—you should read the next section very carefully.

AIDS—Acquired Immune Deficiency Syndrome

What does the term *AIDS* mean? The words *acquired, immune, deficiency*, and *syndrome* are rather technical. What they describe is a disease that people get (*acquire*) that weakens their body's ability to resist other diseases. They are no longer *immune*.

Therefore, they die from diseases that would not normally kill them. The most common of these diseases are a special kind of pneumonia; cancer of the skin, bones, and muscles; and a general weakness and wasting away until the person with AIDS■ has no strength to live.

Some of the symptoms■ of AIDS are swelling glands, loss of appetite, fevers, sweats, fatigue, bleeding, headaches, rashes, coughing, a white coating on the tongue, forgetfulness, and a withdrawal from daily living. It is important to know, though, that a person can have some of these symptoms and *not* have AIDS. Having a sore throat or a high temperature seldom means that you have AIDS.

You don't get AIDS the way you catch colds, or the way, years ago, people got terrible diseases called *plagues.*■ About six hundred years ago, one plague, the Black Death (or bubonic plague), killed almost three quarters of the population of Europe and parts of Asia. The Black Death was spread to people by fleas from infected rats. In those days there was nothing you could do to prevent the Black Death from killing you. And today, as you know, you catch colds, the flu, measles, etc., by breathing germs in the air no matter what you do. However, AIDS is spread only by blood and semen.■ You get it by exchanging blood or semen with another person. *Thus, you "catch" AIDS only by a definite action on your part.* Especially dangerous is *anal intercourse*■ (during which the penis■ of one partner enters the anus■ and rectum■ of another). It is dangerous because there are blood vessels in the rectum and they are very breakable. Thus, semen containing the AIDS *virus*■ can easily get into the blood.

You can also get AIDS in a *non*sexual manner: by sharing needles in illegal drug use, so that blood is exchanged with an infected person. (By the way, doctors and nurses never use a needle on more than one person. They always use a new needle.)

In most cases, you cannot tell whether you or another person is infected with AIDS, unless your blood is tested. People can carry the virus for a long time—even years—and not know it, and yet infect others.

How You Do *Not* Get AIDS

You do not get or spread AIDS■ by hugging, kissing, or eating together, even from the same plates, forks, and spoons. You do not get it by going to school with a person who has AIDS. You do not get it by being sneezed or coughed on by a person with AIDS. You don't get it from toilets, towels, basins, or washcloths. You don't get it from swimming in a pool with a person who has AIDS. You don't get it from garbage in the ocean.

Many people are much too scared that they might get AIDS. Remember, you get AIDS only by definite actions: exchanging blood or semen. The only exception to this is babies born to mothers who have AIDS.

You don't get AIDS from giving blood, and it is nearly impossible to get it from blood transfusions in a hospital. If you need a transfusion to help you recover from an accident or disease where you have lost blood, remember that all blood is tested for the AIDS virus, and the test is very reliable.

Homosexuals and AIDS

In the United States, most of the people who get AIDS▪ are homosexuals.▪ This is because many of them engage in anal intercourse.▪ It is also because gay men tend to have sex with many partners. (This can also be the case with heterosexuals.) In the past few years, however (AIDS was recognized in the USA only in 1981), many homosexuals (as well as heterosexuals) have begun to change their habits. They have sex with only one partner, and both partners get tested for AIDS.

Homosexuals, like heterosexuals, do not spread the disease to others in any way except by sexual intercourse or by shooting drugs with used needles. Therefore, there is no reason to be afraid of homosexual people in ordinary daily life, in the family or out of the family.

A Cure for AIDS?

There is no cure for AIDS▪ yet. If people get AIDS, as you have read, they lose their ability to fight diseases that normally do not harm people, and they die, sometimes in a few months, sometimes much later. AIDS deaths are emotional and tragic.

Doctors and scientists are working hard to find a cure for AIDS, but so far with little success. However, they are learning more about the disease, and perhaps ten or twenty years from now a cure will be developed. By that time hundreds of thousands of people will have died because of AIDS.

Is There "Safe Sex"?

The safest sex is not to have sexual intercourse* at all. But most people when they grow up want to have sexual intercourse. It is safe if they have sex with only one partner who is not infected. Husbands and wives who have been married for years and have had sex only with each other are in no danger of catching AIDS.*

If people who do not know each other have sex, they can help prevent transmitting AIDS, or other sexual diseases, by using a condom* (see Figure 23, page 50). But condoms are not foolproof. A better term for sexual intercourse using a condom is "safer sex."

Remember, *sex* is not a disease! But it can be a way of transmitting diseases. When you get older and decide to have sex, remember what you have read in this chapter, talk with people about it, and *use your head*. Remember the values stated at the beginning of the book, especially information, responsibility, communication, and self-control.

Chapter 12

Some Other Problems Connected With Sex

Sex is one of the strongest forces in human life, and there are other problems with it besides spreading diseases.

Ways to Use Human Energy

Sex is one. Hard physical work is one. Earning a living is one. Thinking is one. Playing music, reading, writing, playing games or sports are other ways. Making friends and enjoying and entertaining them are still others. Traveling, studying, working, caring for a family are all ways of using energy. Too much attention to sex can mean that a person misses out on these other parts of human living and leads an unbalanced, unsatisfying life.

Pretending Sex Does Not Exist

Some people worry so much about the power of sex that they pretend it does not exist. Fifty or a hundred years ago, "nice" people would not admit that they ever thought about sex. Women especially were not told by their parents about this strong force in themselves. A book like this one could not have been written and published.

Even today, many of us have somehow learned to hide our thoughts about sex. You probably know adults who find it very hard to talk freely about sex. You may find it hard yourself. This is a problem.

Language and Sex

It's best when you talk about sex to use correct language. If you and your parents know and can say *penis*, *vagina*, *testicles*, *uterus*, and so on, it is easier to communicate. If you say "my thingy," or "my pussy," or if you talk about the area between your navel and your knees as "down there," it's going to be harder to learn about sexual facts and feelings. It will be harder to communicate.

It's also better to say *sexual intercourse* instead of a "four-letter word" that is slang and shocks people. The same goes for *masturbate* and *anus*. Reading this book with your parents—or leaving it around for them to read—will help you all get used to these correct, factual words and to talk about sexual information and ideas and behavior.

Sex and Being Selfish

Some people want to have sex so much that they will do almost anything to get it. They may say, "I really love you" only because they want a person to have sexual intercourse with them, not because they really love that person. They are telling a lie. Or they might say, "If you really loved me, you'd have sex with me." The answer to that one is, "If you really loved *me*, all of me, you wouldn't say that." No person should have sex with another person unless they both want to do so and have talked about it, and each knows how the other feels.

Adults Who Sexually Molest Children

To *molest* means to hurt or harm. *Child molesters* are people who have sexual contact with children. These adults are confused about sex in their lives. Instead of being attracted to other adults, they are sexually attracted to children and try to have sex with them. This may be because they are mentally sick or very unhappy.

When you know that people sometimes misuse sex, and that some molest children, you are better prepared to deal with these people if they approach you. If strangers offer you candy to get you to come with them, if they ask you to go for a ride in a car, or if they seem to want to touch and pester you, you have to say "No" to them and walk away quickly. If some older person you know tries to touch you more than you like, especially if he or she tries to touch your genitals,* you should not let him or her be alone with you. You should immediately tell your parents or someone else you trust. In any case, you should quickly get away from him or her, whether you are a boy or a girl.

Incest

*Incest** means people in the same family, not husband and wife, having sex with each other. It can be father and daughter, mother and son, uncle and niece, brother and sister, cousins—any close relatives. As with molesters, if someone in your family approaches you sexually, you should leave the person and immediately tell someone. You should do this even though the person who tries to have sex with you, or touches you sexually, says not to tell and threatens to harm you if you do. *Also*, remember that when someone in the family tries to have sex with you, *it is not your fault*. It is their fault. You have a perfect right to have an attractive body, and that body is *your property*!

I must add one point, though. Hugging, kissing, and holding hands in a family are a very good way to show affection and family love. They are quite different from sexual activity and sexual love.

Chapter 13

Different Kinds of Love

The title of this book is *Love and Sex and Growing Up*. Note carefully that it reads love *and* sex. Love and sex are not the same thing. Love is much bigger than sex, even though sex is often a part of it.

So what kinds of love are there?

- Generally, love begins with *self-love*. This may seem strange to you. You may think that people who love themselves a lot are selfish. But those who are really selfish often are those who are not sure of themselves. They are not sure they are as good as they ought to be. Therefore, they cannot give themselves easily to other people. They do not really love and respect themselves enough.

  But think of people who *are* sure of themselves. They know their own value. They are not worried about whether they are good enough.

These are the sorts of people who can love other people, too. They respect the one person they know best—themselves—and they can give the same respect to others.

Children learn *self-respect* or self-love from their families and those close to them. If they love you and respect you, you learn that you are a valuable person. You love yourself and you can love others in turn.

- Another kind of love is *family love*. Part of this is love of parents for their children. Probably you enjoy this kind of love. Parents don't always love everything you *do*. They may even scold or punish you for it, but they keep on loving *you* as their child, as a person.

  And another part of family love is the love of children for their parents. Probably you love your parents but, again, you almost certainly don't love everything they do!

- Yet another kind of love is *close friendship*. This is the kind of love you feel with a very good friend. You are happy when you are together. You can talk about anything and everything. You understand each other well.

- Then there is the love we can call *comradeship*. It grows up between people who are doing a job together that they enjoy. It can be working together for a living—in an office, in a factory, on a farm, building houses, and so on. Or it can be sharing a hobby like music, stamp collecting, mountain climbing, jogging, sewing, or sports.

- One of the most wonderful kinds of love is *love of humanity*, love of all people. Sometimes it is called *brotherly love*, but it includes *sisterly love*, too. If you feel this sort of love, you recognize the special value of every other person in the world, even people you don't know. Love of humanity makes you want to help others, both nearby and far away.
- Then there is *sexual love*, felt by two people drawn together by a strong attraction to each other's body. In this book, you have been reading especially about this sort of love.
- When several kinds of love combine, they may lead to marriage, and we can call this *married love*. The desire to get married often starts with sexual love. It frequently grows into close friendship, comradeship, and family love. (But too often it doesn't grow, and many marriages end in divorce*—see the Word List.)

So you can see that love, and sex, and growing up are complicated and wonderful, but usually not perfect. How well they develop depends on how well you and the people you meet let your lives be guided by the eight values I explained in the preface—not any one of them but all of them:

- the worth of each individual person
- consideration
- the family
- responsibility
- pleasure and good feelings

- self-control
- communication
- information

Now that you have read this book, you may want to talk about these values with the people you live and spend time with.

Word List

This word list tells you the meaning of any difficult word in the book that you might forget as you read. It also contains a few other words that will help you understand the book.

Look over the list and you will see how it is organized. After many of the words, you will find the pronunciation in parentheses: **cervix** (SER-viks). **circumcision** (SER-kum-SIH-shun).
The capitalized letters are the syllables that are accented.

Then comes the definition. If there are drawings in the text to illustrate the word or idea, they are written thus: (see Figure 00, page 00). At the very end of most of the definitions you will find the page or pages on which the word is used in a way that will help you understand what it has to do with love, sex, and growing up.

• • •

abdomen (AB-doh-men). The part of the body often called the belly. It contains several organs, including the stomach, intestines, and bladder. In the female, it also contains the uterus, ovaries, and other organs. Page 2.

abortion (uh-BOR-shun). A way to avoid giving birth to a baby by removing the embryo or fetus from the uterus. Sometimes babies are aborted *spontaneously*, without any action to cause the abortion. Such an abortion is called a *miscarriage*. Page 51.

acne (AK-nee). Pimples, often deep ones, that commonly come with puberty. Usually the condition, caused by an oily substance that clogs the pores, goes away in a couple of years. Pages 35 and 36.

adolescence (ad-uh-LES-ens). Part of growing up. It is the period between puberty and being an adult. Pages 36 and 39.

adoption (uh-DOP-shun). A way that a baby or child is taken into a family. The parents are not the child's natural parents—the mother did not give birth to it—but it legally belongs to the new family and is loved as any other child would be. Page 52.

afterbirth. The materials in the uterus that are pushed out immediately after a baby is born. These include the placenta and the "bag of waters," called the amniotic sac. Page 20.

AIDS. *A*cquired *I*mmune *D*eficiency Syndrome, a deadly disease now rapidly spreading in the United States and some other parts of the world. AIDS is spread by sexual intercourse, and by the exchange of blood by sharing needles when using drugs. Up until now, there is no cure for AIDS, and it ends in death. Pages 54–58.

amniotic fluid (am-nee-AH-tik). The clear liquid that surrounds and protects the baby in its mother's uterus. It is contained in the amniotic sac (see Figure 12, page 17). Page 18.

amniotic sac. See **amniotic fluid.**

anal intercourse (AY-nul IN-tur-kors). Sexual intercourse during which one partner puts his penis through the anus and into the rectum of the other partner, male or female. It is a common way for AIDS to be spread because the rectum contains delicate, breakable blood vessels. Page 55.

antibiotic (AN-tee-by-OT-ik). A medicine used to cure diseases caused by microorganisms in the human body, like syphilis.

antibodies (AN-tee-bod-eez). Minute substances created by the body to help fight some diseases. For example, infection with the AIDS virus results in the production of antibodies, but they do not kill the AIDS virus. A blood test will tell whether or not a person has certain antibodies. If the test is "positive," it means the person is infected with the virus. See also **virus.**

anus (AY-nus). The opening leading from the intestines and rectum to the outside of the body. Bowel movements pass through the anus. The word *anal* refers to the anus (see Figure 4, page 7). Page 6.

bag of waters. See **amniotic sac.**

birth canal. The passage through which a baby is born—the cervix and vagina (see Figures 4, page 7, and 15, page 22). Page 20.

birth control. Control of the number of children born. There are several methods of birth control, including condoms, IUDs, diaphragms, pills, and Natural Family Planning (see Figure 23, page 50). Pages 48–50.

birth control pills. Special pills a woman takes to prevent her from ovulating and becoming pregnant (see Figure 23, page 50). Page 49.

bladder. The sac in which urine is stored. It is emptied by urination through the urethra (see Figures 4, page 7, and 5, page 9).

cervix (SER-viks). The lower part of the uterus. It is like a tube and reaches down into the vagina (see Figure 1, page 2).

cesarean section (suh-ZAY-ree-an). Using surgery to cut through the walls of the abdomen and uterus and deliver the baby without its going through the vagina. A cesarean section is done when a normal delivery might be dangerous to the health of the mother or the baby. (The name is used because of the legend that Roman Emperor Julius Caesar was delivered this way.)

child molester (muh-LES-tur). An adult who molests or abuses children in order to get sexual pleasure. A child should always get away from the molester and tell someone right away what has happened. Page 61. See also **molest.**

circumcision (SER-kum-SIH-shun). A simple surgical operation that removes the foreskin from the penis—usually done when a boy is a few days old (see Figure 7, page 11). Most doctors now advise against it unless it is required for religious reasons, but most boys, no matter what their religion, are still circumcised. Page 11.

climax (KLY-maks). The time or times during sexual intercourse when a man ejaculates semen and a woman's vaginal walls contract several times. It is the moment of greatest sexual pleasure. Page 13.

clitoris (KLIH-ter-us). A small, very sensitive organ just above a woman's urethra. It is covered by lips of flesh called *labia* (see Figure 4, page 7). Gentle stimulation of the clitoris in sexual intercourse or masturbation gives a woman great pleasure. Page 6. See also **vulva.**

conceive (kon-SEEV). To become pregnant. Conception is the moment when the egg is fertilized by a sperm and a baby is started (see Figure 9, page 14). Page 14.

conception (kon-SEP-shun). See **conceive.**

condom (KAHN-dum). A thin rubber device shaped like a finger (see Figure 23, page 50). It is placed over the erect penis before sexual intercourse to prevent sperms from entering the vagina, joining the egg, and starting a baby. Condoms are useful, too, but not foolproof, in preventing the spread of sexually transmitted diseases (STDs). Pages 49 and 58.

contraception (con-truh-SEP-shun). Using a device or method to prevent a sperm from fertilizing an egg and starting a baby (see Figure 23, page 50). Page 48. See also **birth control.**

diaphragm (DY-uh-fram). A contraceptive device in the form of a rubber cap that a woman places in her vagina over the entrance to the cervix to prevent sperms from entering and fertilizing the egg (see Figure 23, page 50). Page 49.

divorce. The legal ending of a marriage. The former husband and wife are now single again—unmarried. Divorce is likely to be hard for the man and woman. It is also likely to be hard for their children, too. It means dividing up the family members and property in ways that are often difficult. But, for all in the family, divorce is often better than going on with an unhappy marriage. Children sometimes suffer because they think they are to blame for their parents' divorce, but that is most unlikely to be true. Page 65.

egg. See **ovum.**

ejaculation (ee-JAK-yu-LAY-shun). The spurting out of semen from a man's penis. Pages 13 and 35.

embryo (EM-bree-oh). The growing fertilized egg during the first two months of a pregnancy. After three months it is called a fetus (see Figure 11, page 16). Pages 15, 18.

erection (ih-REK-shun). The hardening and enlarging of the penis that happens when a man is sexually stimulated, and at other times. Page 12.

fallopian tubes (fuh-LOH-pee-un). The two tubes that lead, one from each ovary, to the uterus (see Figure 1, page 2). The sperms travel up the tubes to fertilize the egg (see Figure 8, page 13). The fertilized egg is moved down the tube to the uterus. Page 4.

family. Parents and their children. Also, several generations of people related to each other: parents, children, aunts, uncles, nieces, nephews, grandparents, and farther back.

family planning. Planning how many children a couple wants to have. Page 48. See also **birth control.**

fertilization (FER-til-ih-ZAY-shun). The moment when a sperm joins an egg and a baby is started (see Figure 9, page 14). It is the moment of conception. Page 4.

fertilized (FER-til-ized). See **fertilization.**

fetus (FEE-tus). What the unborn baby is called from three months after conception until it is born (see Figure 11, page 16). Pages 15 and 18.

foreskin. The skin covering the end of the penis. In most males it is surgically removed by circumcision, usually a few days after birth (see Figure 7, page 11). Page 11. See also **circumcision.**

gay. An informal word meaning homosexual. Page 45.

genes (jeenz). The basic units of heredity. Page 25.

genitals (JEN-ih-telz). The sex organs on the surface of the body, not inside (see Figures 1, page 2, and 5, page 9). Pages 6 and 10.

gonorrhea (gon-uh-REE-uh). A very common STD. Every year there are about two million new cases in the United States. Gonorrhea causes painful urination in men. In women, often there are no symptoms. Gonorrhea can cause arthritis and sterility in women. Fortunately, it is easily treatable and can be cured. Page 54.

groin (groyn). The area of the body where the lower part of the abdomen and the upper, inner part of the legs join. A man's penis and scrotum are in his groin; a woman's clitoris, urethral opening, and vaginal opening, along with the lips that cover them, are in her groin. Page 10.

heredity (huh-RED-ih-tee). The characteristics a child gets from its father and mother when the sperm

73

joins the egg. Inherited characteristics are carried by the genes. Page 24.

herpes (HER-peez). Now the fastest growing STD in the United States. Its symptoms are sores on the genitals. Often herpes goes away by itself, but then it usually reappears. It is incurable and often very uncomfortable. Herpes is rarely dangerous to life, except for babies who are born to mothers whose herpes sores are active. These babies may become blind or have deformed bodies. Therefore, mothers who have active herpes sores should have their babies delivered by cesarean section. Herpes can be spread by warm, moist objects. Page 54.

heterosexuality (HEH-ter-oh-SEK-shoo-AL-ih-tee). Being sexually attracted to members of the other sex. A heterosexual is a person thus attracted (*hetero-* comes from the Greek word meaning "different"). Page 45.

homophobia (HOH-moh-FOBE-ee-uh). A strong, unreasoning fear of homosexuality or homosexual people.

homosexuality (HOH-moh-SEK-shoo-AL-ih-tee). Being sexually attracted to members of the same sex. A homosexual is a person thus attracted (*homo-* comes from the Greek word meaning "same"). Page 45.

hymen (HY-men). The very thin layer of tissue that partially closes the entrance to the vagina. In different women, hymens have openings of different shapes and sizes (see Figure 20, page 39). In a woman with a small hymenal opening, the first sexual intercourse can be painful and cause some bleeding. Using a tampon before intercourse can help a woman avoid this. Page 39.

incest (IN-sest). Sexual intercourse between members of the same family who are not husband and wife. Page 62.

incubator (IN-kyoo-BAY-tur). A boxlike container with transparent walls that provides special protection—air, warmth, and moisture—for a premature baby. Special openings allow the doctor, nurse, or mother to reach in and care for the baby. Page 18.

IUD (*intrauterine device*) (in-truh-YU-ter-in). A contraceptive device, shaped like the letter T or a coil or a loop, made of plastic and sometimes with copper, and placed in the uterus so that the fertilized egg does not implant itself in the wall of the uterus (see Figure 23, page 50). Page 49.

labia (LAY-bee-uh). The lips of flesh that fold over a woman's clitoris (see Figure 4, page 7). Page 6.

labor. The very hard work that the muscles of a woman's uterus, and other muscles, do to push the baby through the birth canal and out into the world. The process is called delivery. (See Figures 14, page 21, and 15, page 22.) Page 20.

lesbian (LEZ-bee-un). A female homosexual. The word comes from the name of the Greek island of Lesbos. Page 45.

"living together." A phrase often used to refer to a man and a woman who share the same house or rooms and have sexual intercourse with one another, but are not married. Sometimes a couple live together as a way to help them decide whether or not to get married.

masturbation (MAS-tur-BAY-shun). Stimulating the sex organs for pleasure. When two people do this together, it is called mutual masturbation. Page 40.

menstrual pad (MEN-stroo-ul). A pad a woman wears between her legs to catch and absorb her menstrual fluid (see Figure 19, page 38). Some people call it a sanitary napkin. Page 38.

menstruation (MEN-stroo-AY-shun). The discharge or flow of blood and lining from the uterus out of the vagina (see Figure 3, page 5). It is *not* bleeding. It occurs about every 28 days. A woman normally does not menstruate if she is pregnant. Pages 5 and 36.

miscarriage. See **abortion.**

molest (muh-LEST). To touch or fondle the sexual organs of a child in order to get sexual pleasure. Page 61. See also **child molester.**

monthly cycle. See **menstruation.**

Natural Family Planning (NFP). A method of birth control that requires a woman to keep very careful records of her dates of menstruation, her temperature, and the mucus that comes from her cervix so that she may know when she will ovulate. She avoids sexual intercourse around that time. Page 49.

navel (NAY-vuhl). The small circular scar where the umbilical cord was attached. Often called the belly button. Page 23.

nongonococcal urethritis (NGU) (non-GON-uh-KOK-ul YOOR-ih-THRYE-tus). NGU is the most common STD in the United States. It can also be transmitted by nonsexual means. It causes painful urination in men, less so in women, because women have a shorter, wider urinary passage. In women there are discharges from the vagina. NGU can also lead to the blocking of a woman's fallopian tubes (see Figure 1, page 2), and cause her to be unable to have babies—to become sterile. NGU is curable by special medicine. Page 54.

ova (OH-vah). See **ovum.**

ovaries (OH-vuh-reez). The two female organs in which the eggs (ova) are stored (see Figure 1, page 2). One egg is released about once a month. This is the usual course of events. In the case of fraternal twins, two eggs are released. Page 2. See **ovulation.**

ovulation (ah-vyu-LAY-shun). The release about once a month of an egg (ovum) from an ovary (see Figure 2, page 3). Page 3.

ovum (OH-vuhm). One of the eggs contained in a woman's ovaries. The plural is *ova.* Page 3.

pad. See **menstrual pad.**

penis (PEE-nis). The main male sex organ (see Figure 5, page 9). A man ejaculates semen from his erect penis. However, most erections do not end in ejaculation. A man also urinates through a tube in his penis. Page 10.

placenta (pluh-SEN-tuh). A spongy collection of small blood vessels attached to the walls of the uterus of a pregnant woman (see Figure 12, page 17). The placenta provides the developing baby with nourishment from the woman's blood vessels and picks up and removes the baby's waste. The food and waste pass through the umbilical cord. Page 18.

plague (playg). A disease that spreads through a population and kills millions of people, no matter what they do, like the Black Death in the 14th century. Strictly speaking, AIDS is not a plague, since you must perform a specific action to get it. Page 55.

pregnant (PREHG-nunt). Carrying a fertilized egg (first embryo, then fetus) in the uterus, where it develops into a baby. A woman becomes pregnant by having sexual intercourse. (See Figure 8, page 13). People sometimes say that she is expecting a baby. Pages 4 and 19.

premature baby (pree-muh-CHOOR). A baby born before the normal end of pregnancy at nine months. If a baby is born as much as three months early, it has a good chance to survive. Page 17.

prostitution (PRAH-stih-TOO-shun). Exchanging sex for money. Women and men who sell sexual services are called prostitutes.

puberty (PYU-ber-tee). The period during which a boy or girl enters adolescence. In a boy puberty is marked by his first ejaculation of semen; in a girl, by her first menstruation (see Figures 17, page 34, and 18, page 37). Pages 33 and 36.

pubic hair (PYU-bik). The curly hair that grows above the penis on a boy and on the upper part of and above the vulva (the vaginal opening and labia) on a girl (see Figures 17, page 34, and 18, page 37). Pages 33 and 36.

rape. Sexual intercourse forced upon one person by another, usually by a man upon a woman. Rape is a violent crime.

rectum (REK-tum). The last part of the intestine, just before the anus. It contains delicate, very breakable blood vessels. Page 55.

reproduction. The process of producing babies.

rhythm method. A method of birth control. The term is now out-of-date. See **Natural Family Planning.**

scrotum (SKROH-tum). The sac of loose, crinkly skin that hangs under a boy's or man's penis and contains the testicles (see Figure 5, page 9 and Figure 7, page 11). Page 8.

semen (SEE-men). Fluid containing sperms. It is ejaculated from the penis during sexual intercourse. Page 10.

seminal vesicles (SEM-ih-nul VEH-sih-kuls). Two small sacs near the end of each vas deferens in a man. Semen is stored in them (see Figure 5, page 9). Page 10.

sex organs. The organs that enable men and women to have children. In women, the sex organs are the ovaries, the fallopian tubes, the uterus, and the vagina (see Figure 1, page 2). In men, they are the penis, the testicles, the two vas deferens, and the seminal vesicles (see Figure 5, page 9). Pages 1 and 8.

sexual intercourse (SEK-shoo-al IN-tur-KORSE). When a man puts his penis into a woman's vagina, and the man and woman move back and forth until the man ejaculates semen into the vagina. It is the way babies are started. Usually, it gives both partners great pleasure. See also **anal intercourse.** Pages 12 and 47.

sexuality (sek-shoo-AL-ih-tee). The sexual nature of human beings. All the things and actions that make us men or women.

sexually transmitted diseases (STDs). Diseases that are passed—transmitted—from one person to another mainly by sexual intercourse. Some of the most common and serious STDs, listed in alphabetical order, are AIDS, gonorrhea, herpes, nongonococcal urethritis, syphilis, trichomonas, and urethritis. For more information about each of them, look them up in this Word List, and read pages 54–58 on AIDS. Pages 53–54.

sperm. The male reproductive cell (see Figure 6, page 10). Sperms are made in the testicles and stored in the seminal vesicles, as a part of semen (see Figure 5, page 9). The plural of sperm can be *sperms* or *sperm*. Pages 4 and 8.

STDs (ES TEE DEEZ). See **sexually transmitted diseases.**

sterile (STEH-rul). See **sterility.**

sterility (steh-RIL-ih-tee). Not being able to conceive children. There are many causes for sterility, some of which are curable. Sometimes the man is sterile and cannot impregnate a woman; sometimes the woman is sterile and cannot become pregnant.

sterilization (STER-il-ih-ZAY-shun). A surgical operation that either prevents a man from making a woman pregnant or prevents a woman from conceiving a baby. See **tubal ligation; vasectomy.**

symptom (SIMP-tum). A fever, pain, rash, etc., that indicates the presence of a disease. Page 55.

syphilis (SIH-fil-is). Syphilis used to be the worst STD in the world and in the United States. Millions of people were crippled by it and died from it, including babies. Fortunately, syphilis is now easily treatable by special medicine, and there are about 40,000 new cases a year in the United States, instead of millions. Page 54.

tampon. A small roll of absorbent material that a woman inserts into her vagina to absorb her menstrual flow (see Figure 19, page 38). Pages 5 and 38.

testicles (TES-tih-kuls). Two oval-shaped organs that manufacture sperms. They are contained in the scrotum. *Testis* (one testicle) and *testes* (two testicles) also are often used. (See Figure 5, page 9). Page 8.

trichomonas (TRIK-oh-MOH-nus). An STD even more common than gonorrhea. It can also be transmitted nonsexually by warm, moist objects that were used by an infected person. Trichomonas causes a smelly discharge from a woman's vagina and itching of her genitals. In men there are no symptoms. It is easily cured by special medicine. Page 54.

tubal ligation (TOO-bul ly-GAY-shun). A surgical operation when a doctor cuts and ties a woman's fallopian tubes so that neither eggs nor sperms can pass. It is a method of sterilization. Pages 51–52.

umbilical cord (um-BIL-ih-kul). The ropelike cord that connects a baby growing in the uterus to the placenta (see Figure 12, page 17). Through it pass food and oxygen from the mother to the baby, and waste from the baby to the mother. Page 18.

urethra (yu-REE-thruh). The tube through which urine passes from the bladder to the outside of the body during urination (see Figures 4, page 7, and 5, page 9). Also, a man ejaculates semen through his urethra. Pages 6 and 10.

urethritis (YOOR-ih-THRYE-tus). Inflammation of the urethra, the tube through which men and women pass urine (see Figures 4, page 7, and 5, page 9). There are many causes of it. It is easily curable but it can come back. Page 54.

uterus (YU-ter-us). The organ in which a fertilized egg grows into a baby, ready to be born. The uterus also pushes the baby out at birth (see Figures 4, page 7, and 14, page 21). And it is the organ that a woman's menstrual flow comes from. Pages 4–5.

vagina (va-JY-nuh). The soft, muscular passageway between the uterus and the outside of a woman's body (see Figure 1, page 2). It is the organ that a man's penis enters during sexual intercourse. It is also a major part of the birth canal. Page 6.

vas deferens (vas DEF-er-ens). One of the two tubes through which sperms pass from the testicles to the seminal vesicles (see Figure 5, page 9). Page 9.

vasectomy (va-SEK-tuh-mee). A method of sterilization of men. It is a surgical operation during which a doctor cuts out a short section of each vas deferens and ties off the ends. This prevents sperms from passing from the testicles to the semen stored in the seminal vesicles (see Figure 5, page 9). Page 51.

virus (VY-rus). A very small germ that passes from one person to another and can cause a disease. Different viruses cause different diseases. For example, the AIDS virus is called HIV (*h*uman *im*munodeficiency *v*irus), and is passed from one person to another in blood or semen. Page 56.

vulva (VUL-vuh). The area of a woman's body that includes the lips that cover the clitoris, and the opening of the vagina. After puberty, the vulva is covered with pubic hair.

wet dream. When a man, or a boy after puberty, dreams about sex and ejaculates semen in his sleep. Page 35.

womb (woom). A common word for uterus, the organ in which a baby grows before it is born (see Figures 1, page 2, and 11, page 16). Page 4.

A Test on Facts

If you want to find out whether you have learned important facts in this book, take this test. If you haven't learned some, read them again (find the page in the index), because correct information is what you need.

You may be using this book in school. Your teacher can use the test to find out if you have learned the material.*

Directions: For each test item, three correct answers are given and one wrong answer.* Find the wrong answer and put an X over its letter on the answer sheet.

---

*(1) Permission to reproduce this test and answer sheet is hereby granted for classes who are reading this book as a part of their course of study.

(2) Research shows that multiple-choice tests that give three wrong answers and one correct answer inadvertently teach children some wrong facts and ideas. That is why this test has the students X out the one wrong answer. The other three correct answers reinforce correct information.

Sample items to show you how to do it:

1. People
   A. have two legs.
   B. are male or female.
   C. can fly with their arms.
   D. grow from babies into adults.
2. The United States of America is:
   A. on the moon.
   B. a nation.
   C. smaller than the sun.
   D. sometimes called the U.S.A.

For these sample items, you would mark the answer sheet thus:

1. A   B   ⊠   D
2. ⊠   B   C   D

because (1) people cannot fly with their arms, and (2) the United States is not on the moon.

1. The following are women's sex organs:
   A. ovaries
   B. uterus
   C. navel
   D. vagina
2. The following are men's sex organs:
   A. penis
   B. vas deferens
   C. testicles
   D. beard
3. Sexual intercourse is:
   A. giving birth to a baby.
   B. the way babies are started.
   C. often a great pleasure for men and women.
   D. when a man's penis enters a woman's vagina.
4. The following are true about eggs and sperms:
   A. An egg is much larger than a sperm.
   B. A sperm can move by itself; an egg must be moved down the fallopian tube.
   C. Neither one can start a baby by itself.
   D. They both look like very small babies.
5. When an egg and sperm join after sexual intercourse:
   A. it is certain that nine months later a baby will be born.
   B. it is called fertilization.
   C. one cell is formed and starts at once to divide and grow.
   D. a baby is conceived.

6. A baby is born:
   A. about nine months after a sperm fertilizes an egg.
   B. every time a couple has sexual intercourse.
   C. when the muscles of the uterus labor to push it out.
   D. through the vagina.
7. Puberty is:
   A. the time when a boy first ejaculates semen.
   B. the time when a girl first menstruates.
   C. the moment when a person becomes an adult.
   D. the beginning of adolescence.
8. Adolescence is:
   A. the time between reaching puberty and becoming a grown-up person.
   B. a time when people don't learn very much.
   C. a period when some boys and girls are more sexually developed than others.
   D. for many people, a difficult time to go through.
9. The following are true about menstruation:
   A. It happens about once a month.
   B. Men find it easier to menstruate than women.
   C. When it happens it shows that a woman is not pregnant.
   D. A woman uses a pad or tampon to absorb the menstrual flow.
10. The following are true about *all* girls or boys:
    A. Boys have penises.
    B. Girls have vaginas.
    C. Girls are timid and gentle.
    D. Girls are female; boys are male.

11. Homosexuals are people who:
    A. have a disease that only mentally retarded people have.
    B. are sexually attracted to members of the same sex.
    C. are often called gay or lesbian.
    D. are found in all areas of life.
12. Birth control means:
    A. using a method or methods of contraception.
    B. that people don't like children.
    C. using a method or methods of family planning.
    D. that people want to plan when to have children.
13. The following are reasons some couples use birth control:
    A. They want to have children but are not able to.
    B. Both the man and the woman have jobs that are more important to them than having children.
    C. They feel they would not do a good job of bringing up children or more children.
    D. They do not feel able to support a child, or another child.
14. The following are true about sterilization:
    A. In men it is done by cutting and tying each vas deferens.
    B. In women it is done by cutting and tying the fallopian tubes.
    C. It is unfair to the other children in the family.
    D. It is a good method of birth control for couples who wish never to have more children.

15. The following are means of contraception:
    A. ejaculation
    B. IUDs
    C. birth control pills
    D. condoms
16. If an adult tries to molest a child sexually, the child should:
    A. get away from that adult.
    B. tell somebody about it as soon as possible.
    C. keep it a secret.
    D. remember that it is not his or her fault.
17. The following are sexually transmitted diseases (STDs):
    A. syphilis
    B. AIDS
    C. urethritis
    D. pregnancy
18. The following are true about AIDS:
    A. Many people are terribly afraid of getting it.
    B. It is spreading rapidly in the United States.
    C. There is as yet no cure for it.
    D. You get it from going to school with children who have it.
19. The following are true statements about love:
    A. One kind of love is sexual love.
    B. Without sexual activity, love would be impossible.
    C. One kind of love is close friendship.
    D. Self-love, or self-respect, is an important kind of love.

Answers to be Xed:

1.	C	11.	A
2.	D	12.	B
3.	A	13.	A
4.	D	14.	C
5.	A	15.	A
6.	B	16.	C
7.	C	17.	D
8.	B	18.	D
9.	B	19.	B
10.	C	20.	D

20. The following are values that this book says are important:

A. information
B. self-control
C. consideration
D. punishment

Index

Page numbers in italics refer to illustrations.

93

Uterus (*cont.*)
  during pregnancy, 20
  See also Menstruation; Placenta

Vagina, 6, 10, 82
  birth and, 20
  intercourse and, 12–13
  opening, 6, *7*
Values, xiv–xv, 65–66
Vas deferens, 9–10, *9*, 82
  and sterilization, 51, 82
Vasectomy, 82
VD (venereal disease), 53. *See also*
    STDs
Virus, 83
Vulva, 83

Wet dreams, 35, 83
Woman
  abdomen, 2
  anus, 6

birth and labor, 19–23
breasts, 19–20, 23
climax, 13, 71
egg (sex cell), 2–4, *3*, 8–9
  fertilization, 4
genitals, 6–7, *7*
  clitoris, 6–7, 71
  labia, 6, 75
  vagina, opening, 6
hymen, 39, *39*, 74
menstruation, 5–6, *5*, 36–39,
    76
pregnancy, 4, 19, *19*
ovulation, 3, 5, 77
sex organs, 1–2, *2*, *3*, 79
  fallopian tube, 3, 14, 26, 72
  ovaries, 2, 9, 15, 77
  uterus, 4–5, *5*, 14–18, *17*, 82
  vagina, 6, 82
urethra, 6
Womb, 83. *See also* Uterus

ABOUT THE AUTHOR

ERIC W. JOHNSON, a graduate of Germantown Friends School in Philadelphia, Harvard College, and the Graduate School of Education, has taught sex education for twenty years in public, independent, and Catholic schools. He is the author of forty-seven books, including *Love and Sex in Plain Language*, *Sex: Telling It Straight*, *How to Live Through Junior High School* and coauthor with Mary S. Calderone of *The Family Book About Sexuality*. He has three grown children, four grandchildren, and lives in Philadelphia with his wife.

ABOUT THE ILLUSTRATOR

VIVIEN COHEN, trained in medical illustration, has illustrated nearly fifty nonfiction books including *The Family Book About Sexuality* and *Dr. Abravanel's Body Type Diet and Lifetime Nutrition Plan*. She lives in New Jersey with her husband and son.